CPA MARKETING

How to Promote Cpa Offers and Make Passive Income

By Jonathan Reilly

Table of Contents

1. What is CPA Marketing?
2. How to Learn CPA Marketing
3. CPA Marketing Strategies
4. Important CPA Marketing Tip
5. Online Affiliate Marketing
6. CPA Marketing Fail
7. How To Implement CPA Marketing
8. Dark Side of CPA Marketing

Introduction

It's never been easier to make money with CPA. What exactly does CPA stand for? It's simply **COST PER ACTION**. You are paid whenever someone completes an offer whether it is a sale or lead using your referral link. There are many CPA companies available to choose from, each having dozens or even hundreds offers.

Throughout this guide I'll be introducing you to a variety of techniques and strategies that you can use to profit substantially from CPA. These are all strategies that I have personally used to make money online with CPA offers. Nothing is left to the imagination.

Upon completing the reading of this eBook you will have a clear understanding of what it takes to profit from CPA offers, and will be able to get started promoting.

What you will learn from this book:

- How to Learn CPA Marketing
- CPA Marketing Strategies
- Important CPA Marketing
- Implement CPA Marketing
- Dark Side of CPA Marketing

Chapter I

What is CPA Marketing?

For the benefit of those of you who do not know what CPA Marketing is, CPA is a short form for "Cost Per Action."

CPA Marketing is different from affiliate marketing (such as ClickBank) in that, it may not be necessary for someone to buy something in order for you to generate a commission. You can generate commissions whenever someone completes an action (that's required by the advertiser) such as filling up a short form (which consists of between 1 to 5 fields), signing up for a free service, or getting free trial to products and services.

CPA marketing isn't marketing done by a licensed CPA or anything like that. CPA refers to "cost per action." So when you see CPA marketing, it is referring to making money online by invoking some sort of action out of your online audience.

An example might be someone clicking on your advertisement for a free product or trial membership and then filling out a short form to receive their free product or membership. In other words, CPA marketing is what the big time media outlets have been using as old-fashioned marketing for years.

The difference is that the Internet has, through hundreds of companies, made cost per action advertising revenue available to everyone with an audience of any size or anyone able to drive web traffic to these CPA offers.

Selling Free Products Is Easy

It is a lot less difficult to "sell" free things to people than it is to convince people to buy something. This is particularly true when you have not established a strong, time-tested trust relationship with your site audience.

Fortunately, many CPA marketers are willing to pay you $1 to get someone to fill in a very short form, rather than spending a dollar or more for every person that actually pays attention to a television advertisement they're running.

This allows the company paying you to get a direct response from its target market for the money it spends. It also helps them to gather details for future contacts with sales prospects. In their eyes this is money well spent.

$1 is only an example, there are some CPA merchants who offer only 5 cents per lead but others who will pay you hundreds of dollars. The difference is typically in the value of the products or services they offer and the percentage of respondents likely to become customers.

You don't have to understand this yourself as a CPA marketing affiliate. You only need to understand that this valuable and legitimate revenue stream is available to anyone.

Successful CPA marketing requires you to be able to leverage traffic. You don't need a website or even a Blog. But the more traffic you can leverage the more money you will make, it is in essence a numbers game.

It starts with you bringing traffic to your affiliate link. You can of course go down the building a website route. When you have a site people love and visit regularly, you are ready to make money via CPA marketing.

In fact, if you have a great website you can do your own advertising to bring people in and use the website to hold them. The more often they come back for free offers, the more money you make.

The amount of money is limited only to the amount of traffic you bring to your site. You may want to take some time to study marketing techniques to drive your traffic numbers up so you can make as much money as possible.

No Website Required

There are numerous techniques available online to push traffic to CPA merchant sites and their offers, pay-per-click, article marketing, media buys, social networking, joint ventures and much more.

The great thing about CPA marketing is that you simply need to find a CPA merchant with a compelling offer and you can start making money the same day. Just utilize the traffic methods mentioned above and push traffic to the merchant.

Since you get paid on a per lead rather than a per sale basis a huge barrier is removed in that your prospect doesn't need to dig out his or her credit card. This is a major bonus as this is one of the biggest stumbling blocks when it comes to online transactions.

Obviously when your prospect doesn't need to make a payment of any kind they are much more likely to do the required action for their free trial/product. Essentially just entering their name and email address in most cases is enough for you to get paid.

CPA Marketing Is All About The Offers

Many people start up CPA marketing and then realize it is harder than they expected. It might be not their fault that they do not achieve huge success in the beginning. CPA marketing is all about numbers and offers. Internet marketing is a numbers' game and you need to get them right. But also, you have to learn the right methods to pick the most profitable CPA offers to maximize your revenue. The truth is that it is more than likely your first few offers you are running are going to flop. But you need to have enough patience to keep on going and test each and every campaign until you find the one that works for you. Here are some tips to help you cut down the time it takes you to find the perfect CPA marketing offers and methods.

Relevancy

It is a common mistake starting up CPA marketers make that they do not choose a relevant offer for their advertising methods. Ensure if you are promoting an offer on channels it is going to be seen by people who are especially looking for that, and not something similar. It is going to increase your conversion rates. For example if you are running a dating website for men there is no point putting up an offer that offers men beauty products, as they are not closely related. But if you are including a free website giving them dating advice they are more likely to be interested.

Network earnings

To make sure you are starting to promote the best converting CPA offers you need to have a look at the network earnings. It is usually displayed in your affiliate area and says: EPC. EPC stands for earnings per click, and the higher the amount is the more profitable to offer is for other affiliates promoting the offer. It is although not a guarantee that you will earn the same amount per click.

The level of involvement

There are three levels of involvement associated with CPA marketing campaigns. There are some easy to convert offers, like email or zip submits, but the payout on these is lower as well. The medium involvement offers are usually the mobile offers that offer downloads, apps or games. And the highest paying ones are the ones that make people take out their credit cards and buy something or participate in a free trial. You are going to see that the more action an offer requires from the visitor the higher the payout is, but the more traffic is needed to get a conversion.

Tracking and tweaking

After you have set up some CPA marketing campaigns you will have to start testing them. If you think you can just set up and go, you are not going to make any money. It is only possible for advanced CPA marketers. Sometimes changing only one word can make a huge difference, so make sure you have a tracking system in place.

Chapter II

How to Learn CPA Marketing

Cost Per Actions/Acquisition (CPA) marketing is an internet marketing technique where an advertiser will pay for a particular action taken simply by a possible client. The payout out of this action is delivered to the affiliate who sent the potential customer to the advertiser's web page if the possible client completes the specified action.

The action can be anything from actually buying something to simply filling in an application. As an affiliate marketer, you can reap the benefits of earning a little commission whenever a customer you send out to the advertiser's web page completes the action. When you have your own website with good traffic, or believe you can set one up, it's not at all hard to monetize it using CPA marketing.

1. Think about searching for an online marketing course at your neighborhood community university or Lifelong Learning center. This is essential if you have never done Online marketing before, as many of the conditions associated with CPA marketing will be unfamiliar to you. In these courses, you shall become familiar with the main types of internet marketing, including affiliate marketing. You can also get an education in online marketing through a number of websites online. Simply make sure the web site is reputable by searching for reviews from former and current users.

2. Consider obtaining an Associate's Degree or Online Certificate in Internet, Digital, or internet marketing. If you wish to build up an excellent knowledge base and you learn best in an instructional

setting, then signing up for a 1 or 2 year program may be your best option. In this program, you shall learn how to start a career as an online marketer, including getting started off with CPA marketing. Like the majority of types of internet marketing, CPA advertising constantly is changing. Those who are most successful are able to learn through error and trial and continuous research into new techniques. It is not essential to have a degree program to become successful.

3. Download an eBook on CPA marketing. Fairly inexpensive (or free) compared to regular books, e-books about technical areas of marketing are very common. Consider titles like "Newbies Guideline to Mastering the Secrets of CPA Advertising," "Newbie 411: The official CPA Marketing Beginners Guidebook" and "CPA Marketing Simplified." Try looking for these titles on a sizable eBook website, like Amazon.

4. Know how you'll make cash. Challenging specific information associated with CPA marketing, it could be useful to have a standard picture of ways to make money doing this. Essentially, you are creating visitors (a flow of people to your site) that you redirect to an advertiser. From there, if this traffic (now potential clients for the advertiser) chooses to opt into the advertiser offer, complete a form, or choose the advertiser's item, you earn a set commission. Oftentimes, this commission could be from $1 to $6 per lead, but in some instances is often as high as $22.

You can still figure out how to achieve success in CPA Advertising without earning a degree in the field. Some of the best CPA Marketers function off the foundation of establishing and nurturing the partnership between themselves (the publisher) and the advertisers.

Learn CPA Marketing Today!

Has anyone ever told you that you should learn CPA marketing if you want to make money easily? If so, did you bother to do as he said? If you did not, let me tell you that you should have done so.

Why? Well, many of the successful internet marketers today are those involved in CPA marketing. Of course, if this is the first time you heard of it, you might not have a clue of how exactly one can make money from it. If you want to find out more about CPA marketing, I suggest you continue reading.

CPA stands for "cost per acquisition" or simply "cost per action" and CPA offers are the offers wherein a user has to fill in forms or download programs from a promoter. These forms to be accomplished could be as short as two text fields for your name and email address, such as those used for newsletter subscriptions, and as long as multiple text fields requiring more personal, residential, and financial information such as the types used for life insurance offers. The examples of programs that can be downloaded through CPA offers are screensavers, wallpapers, toolbars, emoticons and smileys.

Typically, a single email submit is worth an amount from $0.25 - $4.00 and the longer forms are generally worth up to as high as $140. The important thing you must keep in mind when trying to learn CPA marketing is that money comes whenever a user downloads a program or submits a form. Thus, you must focus on getting more users to subscribe to or download your offers. What makes it very appealing is that typically, the users need not pay for anything. In fact, only the users' personal information is needed most of the time. Once the form is submitted or a program downloaded, you earn a commission.

Meanwhile, CPA networks are companies that function as intermediaries between the CPA promoter and the publishers. They host CPA offers from the promoters, have their publishers generate traffic towards these offers and then obtain a percentage of the lead's worth.

The publishers are also called affiliates. Take this example: a promoter pays the CPA network five dollars per generated lead and the CPA network pays the affiliate only four dollars per generated lead, with one dollar taken as a commission cut. This is the way profit is made in CPA marketing.

After you have logged in to a CPA network, you get the ability to look through the CPA offers available and choose which ones you want to advertise. For every individual CPA offer, you will be given a unique affiliate ID for advertising that said offer. It is the CPA network that will track all your generated leads and revenues on your behalf.

What is good about having such a network is that you will only receive a single check for all the commissions you have earned for all the offers you have promoted rather than multiple checks from many different promoters.

You will find many useful resources online that will help you gain a more in-depth knowledge on CPA marketing.

Chapter III

CPA Marketing Strategies

CPA (Cost-Per-Action) Marketing is an internet marketing income opportunity that's very similar to affiliate marketing. The difference between affiliate marketing and CPA marketing is the fact that CPA networks pay you every time a user clicks on your link and takes an action - like filling out their name and email address or download an app on their phone.

The actions required to profit from CPA programs depends on the specific program, but unlike affiliate marketing, CPA programs don't require an actual purchase to be made. This means that it's much easier to profit from CPA programs since users are only required to take a certain action, and then you get paid. With affiliate marketing, the user has to complete a purchase and pay for a product / service before you get paid.

This is only one of the advantages CPA marketing holds over affiliate marketing. It's also easier to convert users with CPA programs since the programs are usually related to global interests - like "Win the brand new iPhone 6s" or "Win a $100 Amazon Gift Card". There's also a lot of different download CPA offers available on different networks. With these programs, your audience needs to download an app or game on their phone for free, and then you get paid for every install you refer.

These are all offers that targets a much more generic audience than a specific internet marketing or weight loss product you'd promote through affiliate marketing.

Now let's take a look at my top 5 strategies for driving traffic and conversions to your CPA offers.

1. Use a squeeze page

The most important part of succeeding in the CPA marketing industry is to make use of a squeeze page. By using a squeeze page, you are increasing your chances for a conversion, while building a list of ready-to-take-action subscribers at the same time.

A squeeze page is a simple "landing page" where visitors will land before they are directed to the CPA offer. Your squeeze page should contain relevant information related to the CPA offer you are promoting, asking users to enter their email address into your email subscription form to continue. Once they add their email to your email list, it will redirect them to the CPA offer. You will need to set up your auto responder to perform these actions.

2. Use Social Media

Social media is a very important part of CPA marketing. Millions of users are turning to Facebook, Twitter, Pinterest, Google+ and other social media networks every day to catch the latest news, check up on their friends, search for coupons and offers, and much more.

This means that it's the perfect place to drop links to your squeeze pages / CPA offers. By promoting your CPA offers on social media, you are tapping into millions and millions of traffic - and if you do a good job, you can drive a lot of traffic back to your links.

The strategy to use here is to first join some groups related to the niche your CPA offer is targeting. If you're promoting a trial offer for a new dieting pill, then you should join health and weight loss related groups / communities on social media.

Once you've joined a couple of groups, start sharing helpful content with the group. Your content should provide some value - do not simply drop links! After a couple of posts, the group members will start to recognize your name and you'll have better authority in these groups.

Now it's time to drop a link to your CPA offer - add a good description and tell the group why they should click on your link. Also add a creative image that is related to the niche you're targeting.

When dropping a link in these groups, be sure to add the link as close to the top as possible without starting the post with the link. Start with a title, drop the link and then add a description.

3. Use Document Sharing Sites

Document sharing sites allow you to share PDF documents with others. They put your documents on their site and anyone browsing their site are able to see and read your documents.

This is another great way to drive traffic back to your CPA offers. By simply sharing a couple of documents related to the CPA offer you are promoting, you are able to drive hundreds to thousands of visitors back to your link, bringing you more conversions and more profit.

You might be wondering what documents you can share here... it's actually quite simple. Do some research about different topics in the niche your CPA offer is targeting. Try to find a few different topics you can target. Then create a simple new document on your word processor and start to write about the specific topic. If you're using a word processor such as Microsoft Word, you can also choose one of the templates that the software comes with to create a nice layout for your document. I usually go with the "Reports" templates.

Add some helpful information in your document - anything more than 5 pages would do. If the information is helping others make a informed decision to the CPA offer you are promoting, the higher the chances of getting more conversions on your clicks. Make sure you add a couple of links to your CPA offer in the document.

Share your documents on as many document sharing sites as you can. Be sure to add unique descriptions for your document on each site, and also include a link back to your CPA offer in each description.

4. Use Instagram

Instagram is a social media network that focusses on multimedia - images and videos. This network is owned by Facebook, and it's almost as popular as Facebook. Instagram received millions of unique daily visitors, and there's millions of new images and videos posted every day.

With Instagram, you can post images and videos, and you can tag them so people can easily find them. You can also like another person's posts, as well as comment on them. The more comments and likes you receive, the better chance your post will go viral.

Instagram also allows you to follow other people, and offers a "timeline" view with the latest posts by the people you follow. The more followers you get, the more exposure your posts get.

Now to drive traffic back to your CPA offer using Instagram can take a while to get started, but once you've tapped into this market, you can drive hundreds of dollars' worth of conversions each and every day from Instagram alone.

To use this method, you should create a new Instagram account. Name your account something that relates to the offer you are promoting. You also need a landing page / squeeze page hosted on a custom domain - you CANNOT link directly to a CPA offer or you will be banned.

Add a profile picture that relates to your niche, and then add a bio that relates to the offer you are promoting. And finally add a link to your squeeze page in the "Website Link" field while updating your profile.

Now you should add only 1 new image / video per day on your Instagram account. You can find millions of images on the internet related to your niche. Tag your image with popular tags. There's many different apps and websites that will give you the most popular and trending tags. Then hit publish.

Once you've added your image, start to follow a couple of people in your niche. Also like some of their pictures, and also comment on some of their posts. Do NOT spam - be thoughtful and considerate, and find a good balance between posting new images / videos, following other people, liking other's posts and commenting on posts.

Continue doing this and you'll soon start building up followers and driving traffic to your squeeze page. Just be-aware that this drives MOBILE TRAFFIC so you need to ensure both your squeeze page and the CPA offer you are promoting are mobile-optimized.

5. Use PPV Advertising

The last strategy I recommend in CPA marketing is to use PPV advertising. PPV advertising is pay-per-view promotion, which means you pay an amount based on the total number of views your ad receives.

This type of advertising works, you just need to find the right network. It will take some trial and error before you finally succeed, but keep at it and you will soon hit your first $100 day.

PPV advertising can cost you as little as $0.01 per visitor, which is really cheap. Imagine being able to convert offers at $0.01 per visitor. That's insane!

The only downside to using PPV advertising is the fact that most PPV networks require a large amount to start with. Most PPV networks will only allow you to start campaign with a minimum threshold of $100. This means you should have some startup capital if you want to use PPV.

If you don't have this much to spend right now, don't worry. There's still an upside to this.

Chapter IV

Important CPA Marketing Tips

1. Work Closely With Your Affiliate Manager

Once your application is approved to join a CPA Network, you will be assigned a affiliate manager who is responsible for your CPA marketing success in that particular network.

If you want to generate a huge amount of profit from these networks, you MUST work very closely with your affiliate manager. Tell your affiliate manager how you will be promoting the CPA offer and they will provide suggestions on which offers will convert best for the traffic generation strategies you are most comfortable with.

Your affiliate manager will provide anything you need to make your campaigns successful. Therefore, it is very important that you establish a solid relationship with your affiliate manager the moment you are accepted into the network.

2. Check Out The Terms & Conditions For Each CPA Offer

Before you start promoting a particular CPA offer, be sure to check out its terms and conditions. Some of them only allow you to use certain traffic generation strategies.

Let me give you an example. Let's say you saw a free trial offer for a weight loss product that you are interested in following. You look into its terms and conditions and discover that you are only allowed to promote this using banner advertising and social networking.

Also, you are not allowed to use email marketing, and Pay Per Click Search Engine Marketing.

Make sure you abide to the terms and conditions very closely. Failure to do so will result in the advertiser stopping you from promoting the offer (and whatever commissions you generate will be reversed - meaning they will not pay you a single cent for the commission you have accrued).

3. Use Only White Hat Techniques

White Hat techniques are basically marketing techniques that are correct and proper. Be sure that, whenever you are promoting any offers on the CPA network, you use only white hat marketing techniques.

The reason is because, when the advertiser find out that you are using any sort of unethical or unauthorized techniques to promote their offers, not only will they stop you from promoting their offers anymore, and that all the commissions that you have accumulated will be confiscated, you will also risk getting banned from the network as a result.

If you have just discovered a traffic generation strategy but you are not sure as to whether or not it is permissible to promote a particular CPA offer using this strategy, always ask your affiliate manager. By doing so, you can be sure that everything you do is correct, and as a result, you will be able to receive your commissions.

By following the 3 tips on CPA Marketing that I have just shared with you, you will be able to experience huge successes in CPA Marketing.

Chapter V

Online Affiliate Marketing

This is about how you can earn commissions with Cost Per Action Marketing as one of your business models with affiliate marketing and making money online today. Cost per action marketing is a lot easier than cost per click and you might find that cost per click might be the way for you to go. For the beginner internet marketer cost per action marketing method is one of the simplest forms of adverting for making money online.

Once you have done some research into cost per action marketing and you feel that it is a suitable marketing strategy for you, then just go for it. This has become one of the most widely used forms of marketing by newbies and well seasoned marketers alike. However, this model is not as easy as some gurus out there lead you to believe.

With new innovative strategies of CPA Marketing, this makes it a well sought after business model these days for advertising online. This method of marketing can be scary at first. But with some education on the subject and with some split testing, you will find that it is quite easy to understand the fundamentals. You will see that this type of marketing has a number of benefits over its stable colleagues of traditional marketing and straight out affiliate marketing.

Cost Per Action focuses primarily on the lead generation part of the business. This has emerged as the preferred way for advertisers to gather leads and build up a database that is more useful in their marketing endeavours later on. If you as a marketer want to improve your existing or establish a new campaign, cpa marketing can provide value for your advertising dollar. When promoting your offer, if the cost of promotion is less than the cpa premium, then you will have made some money.

When comparing cpa marketing with cpc marketing the differences do stand out. The selection process for selecting a cpa marketing niche should involve the same effort as selecting market for your product.

CPA Marketing is a red hot strategy for making money right now and there are lots of people blitzing it right now, making oodles of cash with this business model.

If you are looking for something easy to promote, cpa marketing could be for you. You can start out small promoting zip codes that you can find at many networks.

Internet Marketing Tips - How to Make Money With CPA Marketing

Several internet marketing tips involve using Pay Per Click advertising to drive traffic to your offers. This is a very effective strategy as the traffic will most likely be targeted. However, a downfall to this strategy is that it's becoming harder and harder to use. For instance, Google Adwords, the largest Pay Per Click advertising service, has cracked down on CPA affiliate marketers rather hard lately. If you plan on using this method, it's best you do significant research or risk losing money and getting your account banned.

Another internet marketing tip to drive traffic to your CPA offers is using videos. Video marketing is becoming the mainstream medium on the internet, and it's an effective method for promoting products and services. Therefore, if you have a simple screen capture software, you can create one minute videos showcasing the product or service you're promoting. Then, give a call-to-action in the video as well as provide your affiliate URL in the video description.

These are just a few marketing tips you can use when promoting CPA offers. There are many more strategies to take advantage of, such as blogging, classified ads and article marketing.

One of the most effective ways to improve the ROI of your business is through cost per action or CPA marketing. Cost per Action marketing is a bit similar to Pay per Click; the only difference is its diverse advertising method. To be specific, Wikipedia defined Cost Per Action as an online advertising pricing system where the advertiser would have to pay for a specified action such as a sale or a form completion that was linked to the advertisement.

There are various CPA marketing methods that can be developed to increase the ROI rate of a business. Some of these are: free trial offers, zip code offers, email offers. The most common among these three methods is the free trial offer.

This is used by search engine marketers and online advertisers who choose to provide perks and incentives to potential customers when they sign up for a program. This strategy works both ways because it helps marketers acquire a lead. The customers also benefit by getting the product or a service at a discounted price.

Here are some of a few important benefits:

1. Search engine specialists have option to customize the ad or the campaign based on their target market's demographic profile.

2. A high conversion rate is likely attainable because of the strategic ad copies, geo-targeting options and tactical customization of the target markets' demographic profile.

3. CPA Marketing encourages creativity and analytical thinking because it urges advertisers to perform specific tests before finally launching a CPA program or campaign.

There are many resources online on how one can make money online through CPA marketing. For beginners, type in "Make Money with CPA Marketing" on youtube. There are hundreds of tutorials on this subject.

In this day and age of search marketing, search engine optimization is worthless if the campaigns are not supported by online advertising programs to improve the conversion rate of a product or a service, and this is where CPA marketing comes in.

Quite frankly, it is already being practiced by some search engine marketers by means of email marketing, by using a landing page with call to action and other strategies that attracts their target.

When you bring traffic to your landing page, it brings attention and curiosity. This, in turn influences their decisions to buy a product, to join a program, or to sign up for a affiliate program.

In CPA marketing, there is freedom to create a campaign in a more imaginative way.

CPA marketing is a very effective way to make money online. It does not only improve a brand's name by promoting its services and what it has to offer, it is also a creative way to entice customers to patronize a certain program. It is indeed a must for search marketers and online advertisers to include this online strategy to their marketing campaigns.

Chapter VI

CPA Marketing Fail

CPA marketing is a hot topic. Turning web visitors into money is high on the list for lots of website owners and bloggers. They hear about CPA offers where you don't have to make a sale to make money and it starts to sound really good. There are CPA offers called email submits and zip code submits that just require a small bit of information in order to earn a commission. It seems really simple, but getting it to really work is a different thing.

Not making money with CPA

Getting past the gate keepers at the CPA network is just the start. They have an approval process that may take a few days. They generally want to know how you will be promoting their product. They ask a bunch of questions and you just have to answer the questions they want to hear.

Writing Articles

One of the ways that you can spend a lot of time is writing articles for the directories. This is a free way to get traffic, but it could still lead to failure. They publish your articles and you get traffic to your offers.

The reality might not deliver the results that you want. CPA offers might not last that long. You might be writing articles and the offer disappears. This can feel like a total failure. The other downside to writing articles is doing all the writing and then not getting any traffic at all. You log into your article directory accounts and see that the article that you created is not getting any views at all.

Making Videos

If you don't like writing, videos might be more effective in marketing your CPA offers. They don't require you to be on camera and it doesn't have to take long to create a video. With videos, you still have to do keyword research because it is another free marketing option.

You can fail with videos too. You can make videos, but it doesn't mean that people are going to like them or visit your link. CPA marketers will place a link in the description area that either links back to their websites or even attempts to link directly to the CPA offer.

Blogging

The name of the game is traffic and CPA offers seem like a good fit for blogging. This can work potentially well if you have the traffic. You can setup blogs really easy and adding a simple CPA offer text link is common.

How can you fail at CPA with blogging? It is really easy. Just don't get any traffic to your offers. You can post lots of CPA offers, but without the traffic, you won't see conversions. It won't take too long before you start seeing changes at your CPA network. If you are not providing conversions, the affiliate managers might start to doubt you.

Posting Banner Ads

Failing with banners is simple. People might just ignore them completely. CPA networks might provide you with banners for the offers and some might let you create your own.

People on the web are getting hip to the offers online. They might see your banners and look right through them. How many banner ads have you clicked on lately? The internet public is not falling for the same old advertising anymore. They have to really want what you have to offer.

Social Media

Cost per action offers need traffic and one newer source is social media. The only problem with using social media for your CPA offers is that some offers don't want that kind of traffic. They may have restrictions on how you can promote them.

Domain Forwarding

Another option for marketing a CPA offer is to use domain forwarding. Instead of displaying a long and ugly affiliate link, you instead forward the domain to the link. This looks much better.

Putting a web address that looks professional is an all around good idea. The only place where this can lead to failure is if the offer goes away and you still have the domain pointing to the dropped offer.

You have to monitor the CPA offer emails that your account manager sends. You don't want to waste potential good traffic going to offers that no longer exists.

The key to making money with CPA marketing is bringing in traffic that converts. You have to try different methods to see what works best for you.

Chapter VII

How To Implement CPA Marketing

CPA Marketing is an excellent way to generate revenue on your site. You can accomplish it with three simple steps. Let's get started.

1. Go Find an Offer

The first step is to search for an offer that will bring visitors to your website. There are many different CPA networks to choose from all with hundreds of offers so you should not have a problem finding something that's right for you. You can search based on network, category, price, keyword, etc.

Once you find an offer that seems to match your needs you can then read the offer details. The listings generally offer basic information such as what kind of traffic is allowed or what users are required to do. If it seems like a good match, click the 'landing page preview' button.

Now you will see the pages that your visitors will see when they click the CPA link. If it looks shady, walk away, because it will look shady to your visitors too and the offer will not convert. The more fields on a page the lower the conversion rate so keep this in mind, although more fields compensate with higher commissions. You'll have to weigh it out.

2. Join a CPA Network

Once you decide the offer looks right for you, you need to join the network that runs the offer. To apply simply click the link on the offer page. The application will ask you for your phone number, which they will call you at. For many affiliate marketers this poses a bit of a problem, as we aren't used to talking with others when making money.

You are going to need to get accepted. The CPA network isn't trying to be difficult. They just want to make sure that you are as legitimate a business as they are. Just be transparent. Keep in mind you don't have to be a 'rock star' to get accepted, so if you are new, be honest and tell that you are a beginner.

3. Build Your Website around CPA

After you are accepted to the network, it is time for you to implement your first CPA offer into your website. What's great about CPA offers is that you can have a website that looks like a Fortune 500 Company and you don't waste your time putting up ugly banners that pay hardly anything if at all. There's no need for in your face advertising with CPA.

There you go - three easy steps and you too can be participating in CPA Marketing.

4 Tips to Get Accepted by a CPA Network

There are so many rumors out there about the affiliate community and how it is really hard to get accepted by a CPA Network. Many people feel discouraged before they even start and so they don't even bother. Of course later on they find out it wasn't that hard to get accepted after all. Here are 4 tips to get you accepted by a CPA Network.

Tip 1

Register for a minimum of twice the number of networks that you really want to work with. For example, let's say that you want to start by working with 4 different CPA Networks, and then you need to register to 8 different networks. You will be accepted approximately 50% of the networks that you apply to.

Tip 2

Begin by building your blog. WordPress is a good platform to start with. It's easy to learn and you can easily use open source. It will take a little time to learn it, but there are tons of great tutorials to be found on Youtube. Building your blog can be fun! It's also not quite as intimidating as building a website from scratch.

Tip 3

Begin by applying to the smaller CPA Networks such as Cpagrip or Adworkmedia. If you type in "cpa networks" on google, there should be hundreds of listings right at your fingertip. Focus on the smaller Boutique Networks, where there are fewer affiliates registering, because fewer people are aware of them. They pay attention to the applications they receive and you are far more likely to have a better experience and are more likely to be accepted.

Tip 4

Be determined to get accepted by the network. Only a few Networks process your first application and that's OK just as long as you know that's the name of the game. Accept it and play by their rules. A couple of days after you fill out your first application, if you have not heard anything then find out who their Affiliate Manager is and send them an email. If you are nervous about making phone calls, you still need to build courage to make this one call. It's that important.

Advertise your CPA offers on social media. There are many social media avenues for you to use. One of the most popular is forums, which are part of a CPA strategy. Forums have become very popular with thousands of people visiting them every day looking to learn and share their thoughts and ideas.

Most forums will even allow you to post CPA offers, and many allow you to place a link to your site, so that is a great way for you to start promoting your CPA offers and start making money. You can add a little bit of content as well, so that forum members can read about your CPA offers. When you are done, you can paste your signature profile, which will increase your credibility.

You must make sure that the CPA offer you are promoting is relevant to the topic of the forum. For example, you won't post CPA related posts on an astrology forum if your CPA is about gardening.

Chapter VIII

Dark Side of CPA Marketing

There is a lot of money to be made from CPA Marketing, but there is also a dark side that many people are not aware of. The problem with the CPA industry is that it can be very unethical. There is no formal governing organization to regulate the industry.

There are essentially three distinct groups that make up the relationship of CPA:

- Advertisers
- Publishers (Affiliates)
- Cost Per Action Networks

A CPA Network works as a middleman between advertisers and publishers. The problem starts when one of these groups decides to cheat the others.

Let Me Explain:

If you visit some Forums (usually Black Hat related) you will find many Affiliates showing other Affiliates how to cheat leads out of both the CPA Networks and its Advertisers.

There are many ways to fool or force someone to complete a CPA offer that is not only dishonest but also illegal. Trying to cheat leads from a CPA Network will get you banned, or even worse, you may get Blacklisted from the Cpa network industry.

The Direct Track Platform allows all of the CPA Networks using their System to post their Banned Members for all to see. So if you get banned from one network which uses this Direct Track Platform, you may have difficulty getting signed up to other CPA Networks because your reputation will be known.

The harsh reality is when these Affiliates cheat the CPA Networks this affects other Publishers by a reduced Payout or a higher scrub level (the process of where leads are reversed).

When you join a CPA Network you are essentially putting all your trust into that Network and its tracking system to pay 100% for all the Leads generated.

Unfortunately this is not always the case...

A lot of CPA Networks will shave off leads to ensure that their Profit Levels are kept to a maximum. Most Affiliates do not realize that most of the Cost Per Action Networks using the Direct Track Platform have a built in feature for shaving leads.

This Feature can be set at what ever level they like. For example, they may set it at 10% for a certain CPA Offer meaning the Affiliate will not get credit for every 10th Lead. This is how some Networks pay higher than others because they can afford to by shaving leads.

In order to ensure you get credit for the Leads you generate by your Offers, you must Split Test Different Networks with similar or identical Offers. If one CPA Network offers a higher payout than the other for a specific Offer it may mean that they shave more often than its competitor and overall you may earn more promoting a Survey with a lesser payout as you will not be shaved as much.

I have seen virtually identical CPA Offers on different networks perform very differently using the exact same Marketing Campaigns which means a blatent shaving of leads.

An Advertiser can also shave leads by ensuring that a CPA Networks Pixel is not triggered at certain times. A pixel is either JavaScript or an image tag that when triggered reports back to the Network that a lead has been generated.

"Why wouldn't an Advertiser Shave Leads? It Saves them Money!"

The CPA Industry has already gained the attention of the FTC and the Attorney Generals of many States. Look at the whole recent "ringtones" fiasco that had some CPA Networks paying out as much as $1million to settle lawsuits related to false "free ringtone" marketing.

Most Email Submit Offers put the prospect through co-registration hell by sending many spam related Emails trying to get them to pay for something making the users email account useless because of all the Spam.

Have you ever read the small print on some of these free offers that require an email address? They usually require the participant to fill out three gold offers, two silver offers, two bronze offers and then refer five family members to do the same before they can get the free prize.

"The Small Print is Small for a reason!"

Advertisers can also refuse to pay the CPA Networks for Leads generated which may result in you not getting paid. If you read the

"Terms and Conditions" of the majority of Networks, they indicate that if they are not paid by the Advertiser then you will not be paid.

Stick to the Bigger Networks as they can afford to pay you out of their own pockets if an Advertiser refuses payment.

There are actually CPA Networks who cheat their Affiliates by setting up Similar Landing Pages to yours if they are converting. These CPA Networks have their own in-house Search Team so you are basically showing them what is working for you so they can implement their own and rip you off.

Don't get too close to your Affiliate Manager:

Think about it! If you are making $100,000 a Month on a CPA Network and you have shown your Affiliate Manager your Campaigns, then they will be more than tempted to steal your ideas and make their own money. After all, the CPA Network will not be paying them anywhere near as much as you are earning.

If I were to give you any Advice it would be to make sure your dealing with a CPA Network that genuinely cares about your Business and your well-being rather than how much money you can make for them.

Conclusion

Profits can be made by using smart strategies of CPA Marketing. Online advertising is a large business empire that constantly needs increasing and steady web presence to generate traffic and drive attention to specific products and features that can attract potential customers and buyers. Advertisers online need to have a tactical way of delivering attention to be able to push sales to their market and create profit for the company they are promoting. And so, these online advertisers turn to CPA networks for online advertising and marketing.

If you want to give Cpa Marketing a try, then you should seek to explore, explain, and implement the strategies outlined in this book toso you can acheive real and measurable results. Good luck to all your Cpa Marketing Success!